Atlanta History
For Cocktail Parties

James M. Ottley

Foreword:

In my mid-twenties, I read from cover-to-cover Franklin Garrett's comprehensive history of Atlanta, entitled: Atlanta and Environs: A Chronicle of Its People and Events. I found it fascinating, but realized many readers would not have the time or, perhaps interest, to read the entire text since it is over 3,000 pages long, is comprised of three volumes and contains almost every detail of Atlanta's history. It is truly a work of art and it unequivocally established Franklin Garrett as Atlanta's official historian. I thought it a worthy endeavor to attempt a synopsis of Garrett's work to make the highlights available to readers with a more casual interest in Atlanta history. In this endeavor, I sought to extract what I felt to be the most interesting events and facts with the hope that this might in turn inspire some readers to pick up a copy of Garrett's more scholarly and comprehensive Atlanta and Environs.

The title of this book is by no means meant to trivialize Atlanta's rich history or Garrett's magnificent work. Undeniably, Atlanta and Environs stands unparalleled as the most detailed and comprehensive resource for studying the history of Atlanta and its people. Instead, it is a recognition that this student of Atlanta history will never be able to match the diligence or the passion of Garrett and further that this book does not seek to be measured in the same category as Garrett's work. The stated purpose of this book is to be a moderately interesting account of some of the more unique, odd and even trivial goings-on in Atlanta's history related exclusively from Garrett's account. It will hopefully encourage readers to read Garrett's Atlanta and Environs in whole or in part. The content comprises a series of stories from

3

the first volume of <u>Atlanta and Environs</u> that I found interesting enough or quirky enough to relate at cocktail parties after I had exhausted my insights on the weather. As such, it is not a comprehensive or congruent account of Atlanta's history. I hope to complete a similar compilation from the second Volume.

Because I sought to cherry-pick what I submit as the quirky and interesting of Atlanta history, I was stumped for some time as how to logically organize this sometimes incongruent content into chapters. I finally concluded that there was not a logical way so, accordingly, there are no chapters in this book. This project could not have been organized at all, however, without the help of my diligent and long-suffering secretary, Cheryl Hall King, who converted miscellaneous and random scribbling into legible text and to whom I am eternally grateful. She has probably spent more time on this than I have.

I sincerely hope that you enjoy this collection of factoids, trivia and anecdotes and that you are drawn to investigate Garrett's masterpiece, <u>Atlanta and Environs</u>. All proceeds from the sale of this book will be donated to the Atlanta History Center in memory of Franklin Garrett. I also hope that this survey of certain parts of Atlanta history will engender a desire to know more about the background of our fair city and its industrious people. And if your spouse tells you that you seem to be a little less dull at cocktail parties, then that's all good too.

In The Beginning:

On January 8, 1821, the Creek Indians who inhabited the middle and southern areas of Georgia ceded a large tract of land to the United States Federal government.[1] Atlanta was later created on land granted from this tract. As an aside, the Creeks actually called themselves "Muscogees," but the British surprisingly disregarded their actual, chosen name and called them Creeks by virtue of their tendency to live near creeks.[2]

Out of this 1821 cession, there were five huge counties which were created including Henry County and Fayette County.[3] DeKalb County was carved out of Henry and Fayette Counties in 1822 and Fulton County was later created out of DeKalb County in 1853.[4] Henry County was actually named after Patrick Henry, the famous orator and patriot, and DeKalb County after Baron Johann De Kalb, a native German who was killed fighting for the colonies at the battle of Camden, South Carolina in the American Revolution on August 9, 1780.[5]

Why Every Road in Atlanta is Not Pinetree Street, Pinetree Drive, Pinetree Place, Pinetree Corner, or Pinetree Battle, Etc.:

There were three principal Indian villages in the vicinity of present day Atlanta along the Chattahoochee, the most northerly of which was Standing Peachtree.[6] It was located on the present site of the river pumping station of the Atlanta Waterworks located on Ridgewood Road.[7] Most Indian villages were named for a prominent natural feature and Standing Peachtree was, accordingly, named after a prominent tree.

5

There is an unresolved question though as to whether that prominent tree was a peach tree or a "pitch" tree. Garrett explains that whether it was a standing peach tree or a prominent pitch (or pine) tree has been lost in history and never definitively determined.[8] He explains that there are two stories about the tree which might tend to indicate that the tree was actually a pine tree. One account provides that the tree was unique or prominent by virtue of a marking or blaze and that the Indians had blazed the tree to extract its rosin or pitch.[9] There is also an account that lightning struck the tree, causing the sap to run down the trunk which made it stand out. This would tend to indicate it was a pitch tree.

But Garrett also directs the reader's attention to an 1897 interview of one George Washington Collier whose federal mail route took him through Standing Peachtree. Mr. Collier stated in the interview that there was in fact a large mound of earth at the site and a large peach tree growing atop the mound.[10] Garrett ultimately submits that, even though a pine tree might be more logical, given the plethora of pine trees in the region, the historical written records support the peach tree designation. He cites the fact that "Pitchtree", as a designation, has not survived in "a single record, document or place name, past or present."[11] The name Peachtree has, of course, been prolifically repeated and recorded, the earliest written reference being in a letter dated May 27, 1782, written by a J. N. O. Martin who wrote of a rendezvous of the Cowetas "at the Standing Peachtree."[12]

The Origin of Peachtree Road:

During the war of 1812, the Creeks allied with the British and the State of Georgia built a string of forts to defend against them.[13] Two of these forts were Fort Peachtree, which was built at the Standing Peachtree and the other, named Fort Daniel at Hog Mountain which was located in Gwinnett County.[14] Garrett is not specific as to the exact location of Hog Mountain. A road was built spanning the 30 mile distance between these two forts in 1814 and became the original Peachtree Road and was named Peachtree Road from the very beginning.[15]

The Georgia Canal Prospect:

In 1825, the Georgia Legislature created a Board of Public Works to provide a system of internal improvement, such as canals, railroads and roads.[16] Hamilton Fulton, was appointed as Chief Engineer.[17] He was a middle-aged Scotchman who had spent most of his life in England but had recently been working in North Carolina.[18] Garrett writes "[t]he Board planned two major projects, one to traverse the state from the Tennessee [River] to the Atlantic, and the other from the Savannah [River] to the Flint [River]."[19] In the summer of 1826, Fulton and Wilson Lumpkin, future governor of Georgia, made a survey between the Tennessee and the Atlantic for a possible canal route or railroad route.[20] But Lumpkin determined "[a]fter laborious and instrumental examination of the country from Milledgeville to Chattanooga,…that a railroad could be located to advantage between the two points above named, but that a canal was impracticable."[21] One can only surmise that Atlanta's current water shortage issue might have been a nonissue had a canal been built between those points. The plans were dropped altogether in 1836, however, due to a lack of public support.[22]

Famous and Sundry Place Names:

Decatur actually predated Atlanta and was incorporated on December 10, 1823, long before Atlanta was created.[23] It was named after Stephen Decatur, a naval officer who made history during the war against Tripoli in 1804 and in the War of 1812.[24]

The original name of the town of **Stone Mountain** was "New Gibraltar" and was incorporated under an act of the General Assembly on December 21, 1839.[25] In 1847, the name of the town was changed to Stone Mountain.[26]

Piedmont Road was originally called "Plaster's Bridge Road."[27] Plaster's Bridge crossed Peachtree Creek two to three hundred feet downstream from the current bridge. Benjamin Plaster, Sr.'s home was located at the southeast corner of the intersection of Lindbergh Drive and the Southern Railway, and he is actually buried in an unmarked grave several hundred feet south of that home in the right angle formed by Peachtree Creek and the Southern Railway line. He owned 1,316 acres which included the present sites of Peachtree Hills Park, Peachtree Heights and the eastern part of Brookwood Hills.[28]

Cherokee County gets its name from the Cherokee Indians who inhabited north Georgia and who were removed from the area.[29] Georgia officially took possession of Cherokee County on May 24, 1838.[30] Garrett writes that the Cherokees were gathered into collection camps near Dahlonega, Ellijay and Canton among other towns.[31] It appears to have been a massive and tragic operation as "[a]pproximately 15,000 Indians were removed from Georgia in 1838" and over 400 died en route to Arkansas.[32]

On April 16, 1839, Hardy Pace, the proprietor and namesake of **Pace's Ferry** and also a postmaster, moved across the Chattahoochee "to the present site of Vinings in order to be on the W. & A. Railroad."[33] "The name of the [post] office was changed to Cross Roads."[34] This settlement later became known as Vinings Station for one of the engineers who built the railroad.[35] In 1904, the name was changed to **Vinings**.[36]

In August of 1854, Thomas Moore built a grist mill on Peachtree Creek, a short distance above Nancy Creek.[37] Although burned by arson in 1861, it was rebuilt and operated until 1901 when the site was no longer suitable for a gristmill, a city sewage disposal plant having been built upstream.[38] Bummer. **Moore's Mill Road** gets its name from the mill and a segment of the road actually formed part of the original Peachtree Road which connected Fort Daniel at Hog Mountain in Gwinnett County to Fort Gilmer at the Standing Peachtree.[39]

East Point sprang up at the eastern terminus of the Atlanta and West Point Railroad as it was being built.[40] Garrett writes that "strangers to Atlanta never cease to wonder why one is compelled to pass through West End in order to reach East Point."[41]

In April of 1852, Clark Howell, an Atlanta councilman, left his post and moved to land he had recently acquired on Peachtree Creek.[42] He built a "grist and sash" sawmill known as **Howell's Mills**.[43] Howell's Mills actually became a U.S. Post Office on February 29, 1876, with Mr. Howell serving as postmaster and it served as a post office until 1891.[44] The original Howell Mill was "situated in low ground on the north bank of Peachtree Creek just downstream from the present…bridge."[45] The mill was accidentally destroyed by fire in the late 1870's and Mr. Howell moved back to Atlanta.[46] Although there seems to have been some confusion on the subject, Garrett sets the record straight that "[t]he old stone building on the west side of Howell Mill Road, just south of Peachtree Creek, now incorporated in a residence, was *not* part of Howell's Mill."[47] [Emphasis added]. Instead, it was a unit of a woolen mill established by the Foster Brothers, of Madison, Ga., in the early 1880's."[48]

Private residence on Howell Mill Road which was a woolen mill owned by the Foster Brothers; it was not Howell's Mill.

Later Charles A. Howell established another Howell's Mill on Nancy Creek, on property currently owned by The Westminster Schools. As of 1954, the miller's small brick house was still standing[49], but does not appear to be in existence as of the date of this study.

The county of **Milton** was created by act of the Legislature from parts of Cherokee, Forsyth and Cobb Counties on December 18, 1857.[50] It was named in honor of John Milton, Georgia's first Secretary of State and the man who preserved Georgia's records during the American Revolution.[51] **Alpharetta**, coined from the first letter of the Greek alphabet, was named the county seat of Milton.[52] Milton was later merged with Fulton County on January 1, 1932.[53]

Clayton County was created out of Henry and Fayette Counties by act of the Legislature on November 30, 1858.[54] It was named for Judge Augustine Smith Clayton (1783-1839) of Athens, Georgia, a distinguished jurist and statesman.[55] Jonesboro was named the county seat.[56] The original name for **Jonesboro** was Leaksville, but with the arrival of the Macon and Western Railroad in the mid-1840's civic pride was on the upswell and no one was particularly proud of the name Leaksville.[57] The city was renamed Jonesboro in honor of Samuel G. Jones, one of the builders of that railroad.[58]

Edgewood was incorporated on December 9, 1898. It was called Edgewood because it was on the "edge of Atlanta."[59] On January 1, 1909, it was incorporated into the City of Atlanta and lost its independent identity.[60]

Atlanta's First Home:

In 1833, Hardy Ivy, a native of South Carolina, became the first white settler to build his own home within the present area of downtown Atlanta, but he was not the first person to settle in that area.[61] He purchased his land and agreed to make installment payments equal in value to $225.00 in the form of produce "as he could afford it" for Land Lot 51 of the 14th District.[62] The area is delineated by the following present day boundaries: "North, by a line running east and west between Baker Street, N.E., and Forrest Avenue, N.E.; South, by Edgewood Avenue; East, by Fort Street, N.E., and West by Peachtree Street."[63] In the center, on high ground he constructed a log cabin.[64] Taxes on his land in 1843, the year after he died, were fifty-five cents.[65]

Map showing approximate present day boundaries of land settled by Hardy Ivy, the first person to build a home in downtown Atlanta.

The Events Leading to the Creation and Location of Atlanta:

In 1835, leaders in South Carolina began the "promotion of a railroad to connect Charleston with Louisville and Cincinnati on the Ohio River."[66] Governor Lumpkin of Georgia was worried that Georgia would not participate and warned the Legislature of his concerns.[67] That railroad was built and did bypass the State of Georgia completely. Not wanting Georgia to miss out on such an important wave, in December of 1836, the Legislature and the new Governor, William Schley, authorized the construction of a railroad "from some point on the Tennessee line near the Tennessee River...to some point on the southeastern bank of the Chattahoochee River and which shall be most eligible for the extension of branch railroads thence to Athens, Madison, Milledgeville, Forsyth, and Columbus, and to any other points...as the most proper and practicable...."[68] Georgia thus embarked on its own state railroad with the hope that other private roads would pay to connect up with it. It was to cross the Chattahoochee "at some point between Campbellton, in Campbell County, and Wynn's Ferry in Hall County."[69] Garrett notes that these points are 70 miles apart.[70] The railroad was to be called "the Western and Atlantic Railroad of the State of Georgia."[71] Garrett further notes that the 1826 survey of Hamilton Fulton referenced earlier "finally bore fruit."[72]

There were originally six sites chosen for the crossing of the railroad over the Chattahoochee River.[73] The choice, of course, would in turn determine the future site of Atlanta. Work began on the railroad and a benchmark was placed two miles below Pittman's Ferry in Gwinnett County at the present Medlock Bridge.[74] From that location, the engineers then tried

13

to chart a route to the Etowah River but could not achieve the gradients specified for the railroad line.[75] Accordingly, the Pittman Ferry route was scrapped, and the river crossing was set "upon the precise spot where the old Dixie Highway No. 41…spanned the river."[76] To avoid a sharp curve, it was later relocated in 1850 to a point 800 feet downstream.[77] The 1836 Act authorizing the railroad did not provide for the railroad to extend beyond the southeastern bank of the Chattahoochee, but at the same time, terminating it there did not comply with the portion of the Act reading "which shall be most eligible for the extension of branch railroads thence to Athens, Madison, Milledgeville, Forsyth, and Columbus, and to any other points…as the most proper and practicable…."[78]

Stephen Harriman Long, the chief engineer of the project, then assembled a report to the Legislature which provided in part that extending the line another eight miles would comply with the requirements of the Act to make the line "eligible for the extension of branch railroads thence to Athens, Madison, Milledgeville, Forsyth, and Columbus, and to any other points…as the most proper and practicable…."[79] The Legislature agreed and amended the Act in 1837 accordingly.[80] The original benchmark, which was later moved, was where "Foundry Street crosses the W. & A. tracks."[81] The southern terminus of the Western and Atlantic Railroad and the settlement which grew up around it was known, unofficially, for several years as "The Terminus" or "Terminus.[82] This was a slightly different location from the final end point selected for the railroad.

The issue of extending the final location of the Western and Atlantic Railroad ("W. & A."), and consequently the future location of Atlanta, was

14

debated several times between 1838 and 1842.[83] In 1838, a bill was introduced in the State senate to extend the southern terminus *all the way into Henry County* but the bill was voted down.[84] The chief engineer of the Monroe Railroad, another railroad being constructed in the area, was adamantly opposed since it had paid $25,000.00 to construct an embankment to carry its tracks over low ground to connect its northern terminus with the original proposed southern terminus of the W. & A.[85]

In 1841, the chief engineer of the W. & A. received instructions from the W. & A. Board of Commissioners to slightly extend the railroad to a point "suitable for the erection of depot, buildings, etc."[86] The president of the Monroe Railroad, again trying to protect its $25,000.00 embankment investment, protested to the Governor, who then wrote a letter to the W. & A. chief engineer and asked him to halt further action until the matter was put to the Legislature.[87] This time it was a matter of 1,200 feet.[88] The issue was almost never resolved. Interestingly enough, the location of the terminus was, according to Garrett, apparently "overshadowed by the larger question of whether or not the *entire State Railroad enterprise should be dropped.*" [Emphasis added].[89] It is reasonable to conclude that with no state railroad, there would have been no terminus, and therefore no Atlanta. Given Atlanta's massive size today and the significance of its economic impact on the region and the nation, it is hard to believe that it came perilously close to never existing at all.

In 1841, an Act was passed that, among other provisions, did away with the W. & A. Board of Commissioners.[90] In lieu of the Board, former Governor Wilson Lumpkin (Governor of Georgia from 1831 to 1835) and

Charles F. M. Garnett were appointed disbursing agent and chief engineer, respectively.[91] It was these two men that determined the final terminus location sometime between February 7 and July 11, 1842,[92] thus making perhaps the most significant decision in the entire history of Atlanta real estate. The final terminus of the W & A was set at the "site of the former Union Station between Pryor Street and Central Avenue."[93]

Map with arrow indicating the final terminus selected for the W. & A. Railroad between Pryor Street and Central Avenue, and consequently, the birthplace of the great city of Atlanta.

A deed was delivered for the property on July 11, 1842, by Samuel Mitchell of Pike County which is addressed below.

In a letter to his daughter Martha 11 years later, Governor Lumpkin confirmed that the location was "entirely selected by Charles F. M. Garnett...and [himself]."[94] He wrote that as soon as the site was selected, he immediately wrote to Mr. Mitchell (the owner), and sent the communication by a trustworthy express "informing him of his interest in purchasing the property and requesting that Mr. Mitchell visit him in Marietta to consummate the sale."[95] The time-honored sport of speculating on Atlanta real estate was born. Governor Lumpkin states in his letter that the speculators got to Mr. Mitchell about the same time, but that Mr. Mitchell was "too much of a gentleman of too much intellect and character to have been imposed upon by such fellows."[96] Governor Lumpkin also wrote that he never knew how the speculators found out the location selected.[97]

Mr. Mitchell was apparently a savvy real estate man himself. He insisted on donating the land and stated that it was an honor for him to do so.[98] Governor Lumpkin wrote that consequently he "therefore took only five acres, what was necessary for present purposes, and…must confess [Mitchell's] cleverness and liberality influenced him to take less land than he [Lumpkin] should have done" had the state had to pay for it.[99] Mr. Mitchell obviously realized that his surrounding property would skyrocket in value after construction began and it was more profitable to give the State a small parcel rather than sell it a larger parcel at pre-development prices.

There was considerable controversy involving the site selection as there was an inquiry into the matter by the Hopkins Commission in 1895.[100] Garrett writes that the controversy was closed without any findings of wrongdoing on the part of Garnett and Lumpkin.[101] Garrett explains the basis of the controversy as follows:

> [O]ne is led to wonder why it was necessary to extend the W. & A. into Land Lot No. 77 at all. Long and Brisbane had determined five years before that Land Lot 78 met every requirement for both a terminus and a junction. The point they selected was on a ridge. There was plenty of space

17

available in Lot 78 and no evidence to indicate that Reuben Cone, the owner, would not sell all that was needed. The Monroe Railroad spent a large sum to make a connection at the original location. The change was not made to accommodate the Georgia Railroad. That line had already been surveyed by L. P. Grant, of its engineer corps, to a point near the present Broad Street bridge. Indeed, to make the Mitchell lot serviceable, two major pieces of construction were required--one, a deep cut had to be excavated at the present Broad Street bridge site, and a considerable fill was necessary in the low swampy area of the State Square. Whatever the reason, those concerned have left us in the dark except to say that space was needed for depots, buildings, shops, etc. Yet the only buildings the W. & A. erected in Lot 77 were a passenger depot and a two-story frame office building. Its shops and roundhouse were established in Lot 78 under and contiguous to the present Spring Street viaduct.[102]

The Roswell-Roosevelt Connection:

Roswell King was a prosperous planter in South Georgia and for some years manager of a plantation on St. Simons.[103] In 1837, he traveled to Dahlonega, Georgia to visit the new U.S. Mint at the request of officials of the Bank of Darien.[104] Upon arrival at the Chattahoochee, he was impressed with the area and thought it would make a "pleasant site for a town."[105] He also noted there was "abundant water power for manufacturing establishments."[106] Not long thereafter, Mr. King, together with family and friends from the low country, came to the area where the city of Roswell, Georgia now sits and founded the town.[107] Some of the settlers intended to only reside there during malaria season, but liked the area so much they became permanent residents.[108]

Major James Stephen Bulloch was one of the original founders of Roswell, Georgia.[109] Major Bulloch's daughter, Mittie, married Theodore Roosevelt, Sr. and became the proud parents of President Theodore Roosevelt.[110] Yet that was not the only Roosevelt with ties to Roswell, Georgia. Another son of Mittie and Theodore, Elliott, was the father of Eleanor Roosevelt.[111]

The Birth of Buckhead:

Daniel Johnson deeded 202.5 acres (then in DeKalb County) to Henry Irby on December 18, 1838 for $650.00.[112] Interesting trivia, Mr. Irby was a small man and wore a No. 6 boy's shoe.[113] Notwithstanding his shoe size, Mr. Irby left a huge footprint on the history of Atlanta. Shortly after purchasing the property, again 202.5 acres of Buckhead real estate for $650.00, Mr. Irby erected a tavern and grocery at what is now the northwest corner of West Paces Ferry and Roswell Roads.[114] Garrett writes that in early 1840, someone, maybe even Mr. Irby himself, shot a buck at a spring just south of Paces Ferry Road and a few hundred feet west of Peachtree Road.[115] The head was mounted on a post, not at the above-referenced corner, but at the spring, and the locality became known as Buckhead.[116]

Through the years there have apparently been attempts to change the name.[117] "Northside Park" was suggested at one point but never implemented.[118] Attempts were also made to designate Buckhead as a post office, but this was never accomplished because of the existence of a

Buckhead post office in the town of Buckhead, Georgia in Morgan County.[119]

Mr. Irby died February 20, 1879 at the age of 72 and is buried in the Sardis Methodist Church graveyard on Power's Ferry Road.[120]

Sardis Methodist Church on Power's Ferry Road with cemetery to the left where Henry Irby was buried.

Buckhead suffered its first homicide on Christmas day in 1856.[121] Foreshadowing future bar homicides to occur there, a sizeable crowd had gathered around the tavern. An argument arose between Henry Norton and Henry Irby, both unarmed, about whether Mr. Irby had paid his money for a raffle.[122] George W. Irby, Henry Irby's son, came running up to the crowd and fired a pistol at Mr. Norton who died from the wound.[123] George Irby was only 13 or 14 at the time. He was found guilty of manslaughter and sentenced to two years hard labor.[124]

Atlanta's Prior Name:

As to the naming of Atlanta, Governor Lumpkin wrote to his daughter Martha in 1853, that Mr. Mitchell (the owner of the land where the terminus was located) and many others wanted the town to be called Lumpkin after himself.[125] Governor Lumpkin would not allow it though because there was a Lumpkin County and a village of Lumpkin that were already named after him.[126] Governor Lumpkin thought it should be called "Mitchell" after Mr. Mitchell.[127] Mr. Mitchell and engineer Garnett, with whom Governor Lumpkin selected the site, decided the town should be called "Marthasville" in honor of Governor Lumpkin's youngest daughter.

Atlanta Anomalies:

None of the downtown streets in Atlanta run directly due south, north or due east or west.[128] When the five acres of the State Square (the name given to the original five acres donated by Samuel Mitchell) were surveyed, "the present boundaries of which are Decatur Street on the northwest; Alabama Street, southwest; Pryor Street, northeast, and Central Avenue, southeast, the north line and south line were drawn parallel to the railroad right of way."[129] The streets were then platted parallel with the four sides.[130]

Map showing current day boundaries of original 5 acre State Square from which Atlanta grew.

Although probably noticed by a few, today the unusual width of Marietta Street between Peachtree Street and Spring Street has an interesting story behind it. A certain Judge Reuben Cone, originally from Decatur, moved to Atlanta in the mid-1840's and constructed a residence on the north side of Marietta Street between what is now Fairlie Street and Cone Street.[131] He was unable to see the post office from his front veranda, so he had the road widened between his house and the post office which was located at the 'point' of Five Points.[132] Five Points, at the time, however, was actually just "two points", the intersection of Decatur and Peachtree Streets. Once the road was widened, the postmaster could give him a signal at mail time to tell him whether or not he had any mail, "thereby saving many unnecessary steps" to the post office.[133] As an aside, Judge Reuben Cone was born in Connecticut in 1788, and moved to DeKalb County in time to become one of the original commissioners of the town of Decatur in 1823.[134] He later moved to Atlanta in the mid-1840's having previously acquired much of the land on which it was built.[135]

A bird's-eye view of Marietta Street (right half of picture) showing its greater width between Peachtree and Cone Street.

Atlanta Firsts:

On April 24, 1871, what appears to be the *first Atlanta historical society* was formed called the "Atlanta Pioneer and Historic Society."[136]

The first locomotive to run on the W. & A. was the "Florida." It was purchased from the Georgia Railroad which ended at Madison, Georgia.[137] The locomotive was driven to the end of the line at Madison, Georgia, then loaded onto a huge wagon drawn by 16 mules and brought up through Decatur to Marthasville.[138] The W. & A. at the time was not yet connected to any other railroads.[139] A single passenger car, built at the state penitentiary in Milledgeville, was also hauled in similar fashion to Marthasville.[140] The Florida and this passenger car constituted Atlanta's first train.[141]

General William T. Sherman's first visit to the area was in 1844, and was significantly less eventful than his visit in 1864. As a 23-year-old First Lieutenant in the U.S. Army in Charleston, he received orders to report to Marietta, Georgia.[142] He took the train to Madison, Georgia, then took the mail coach through Marthasville arriving in Marietta on February 17, 1844.[143] He spent the next six weeks "taking depositions in upper Georgia and Alabama concerning certain losses by volunteers in Florida of horses and equipment by reason of the failure of the United States to provide sufficient forage."[144] According to Garrett, in Sherman's spare time, he "repeatedly rode horseback to Kennesaw Mountain, from the summit of which he viewed the surrounding country."[145] After completion of his work, he was then transferred to Bellefonte, Alabama where, en route, he also familiarized himself with the area west of Marietta and around Rome, useful information he would draw upon twenty years later.[146]

Atlanta's first amusement park boasted the first 'pre-Ferris' Ferris Wheel. Anderson W. Walton, one of Atlanta's six original councilmen, owned approximately three acres located along Walton Street at the northwest corner of Spring Street.[147] There was a spring called Walton Spring on the low-lying part of the property after which Spring Street is named.[148] Walton Spring was a "noted resort in early Atlanta."[149] Garrett writes that it was in connection with Walton Spring that "Atlanta's first amusement park came into being."[150] Between the spring and Peachtree Street, Antonio Maquino had a wagon yard and sold drinks and knickknacks.[151] To bring in more business, he designed and constructed a large vertical wooden wheel forty feet in diameter which would carry the adventurous on a 'pre-Ferris' Ferris Wheel ride.[152] He attached two dry goods boxes to the wheel for seating compartments and powered the rotating wheel by two men.[153] Mr. Maquino's wheel preceded the famous Ferris Wheels of Paris and Chicago by 40 years.[154]

The first prison in Atlanta was erected in 1848 on the west corner of Pryor and Alabama Streets.[155] The primary purpose of the jail was for runaway slaves.[156] It apparently had its own unique early release program. If there were enough prisoners being held at one time, they would merely lift up one side and crawl out, the total square footage of the structure being only approximately 64 square feet.[157] Sometimes cohorts from the outside would effect a jail break by lifting the building up off its foundation to allow the inmates to crawl out.[158]

Atlanta's original city hall was built on the present site of the State Capitol Building.[159] It was built in 1854, survived the Civil War, and was demolished in 1884 to make way for the Capitol Building.[160]

Atlanta's first corporation was the Atlanta Gas Light Company.[161] Until 1855, Atlanta only had two utilities, railroad and telegraph.[162] The Atlanta Gas Company was incorporated by the State Legislature in 1856.[163]

The first national bank in the South was organized in Atlanta almost as soon as Congress authorized national banks. The Act of Congress providing for the incorporation of national banking associations was passed on June 3, 1864.[164] Shortly thereafter on September 2, 1865, the Atlanta National Bank was organized.[165] It received its charter and began to operate on December 19, 1865.[166] It was the first national bank to operate in the South.[167] In 1924, the Atlanta National Bank, and the Lowry National Bank merged as the Atlanta and Lowry National Bank; and in 1929, this bank and the Fourth National Bank merged to form the First National Bank of Atlanta.[168] First National was later bought by Wachovia on December 12, 1986.

Atlanta's first all direction expansion occurred on March 12, 1866, with an Act of the Legislature providing for the expansion of the city limits so as to measure 1.5 miles in every direction.[169] "It was the first time the original mile circle of 1847 had been generally extended in all directions."[170]

Atlanta Becomes "Atlanta":

The name change to Atlanta occurred sometime between September 15 and October 15, 1845.[171] The superintendant of the Georgia Railroad, Richard Peters, initiated the change, but he could not think of a suitable replacement, so he asked his friend and associate, J. Edgar Thomson, Esq. for ideas.[172] J. Edgar Thomson was the Chief Engineer of the Georgia Railroad from Augusta to its junction with the W. & A. in Marthasville (n.k.a. Atlanta).[173] One of Richard Peters' duties was to "arrange freight lists, and to notify the public of the opening of the road from Covington to Marthasville."[174] In a letter to a colleague dated May 9, 1871, Mr. Peters wrote that he "was not satisfied with the name given [to a place] that, even at that early day had [been]…prophecied [to be] a great city in the future."[175] Garrett writes that Mr. Thomson came up with 'Atlanta', which was "a coined word, ostensibly the feminine of 'Atlantic' from the Western and

Atlantic Railroad."[176] [Emphasis added]. Mr. Peters approved and issued the circulars adopting the name apparently for the depot only, not the incorporated city itself and distributed them throughout Georgia and Tennessee.[177]

There were apparently protests, namely for the reason that the railroad authorities had no authority to change the name of a city incorporated by the State Legislature, but the protests dissipated since the circulars "did not purport to be an official city document," and since there were "no laws against a railroad naming its depots in any manner they chose."[178] The name caught on however, because at the next session, the State Legislature amended the act of incorporation to replace the name "Marthasville" with "Atlanta."[179]

There were some publications at the time that printed the name as "Atalanta."[180] Knowledgeable in Greek mythology, some editors evidently thought the name "Atlanta" was a typo when they encountered it, and was supposed to be "Atalanta," the goddess of fleetness and strength.[181] Instead of "Atlanta" they printed it as "Atalanta."[182] Interestingly enough, the creator of the name of the great city, J. Edgar Thomson, was never a permanent resident of Atlanta.[183]

Former Governor Lumpkin, took offense at the name change, writing to his daughter Martha in a letter dated October 25, 1853, that "[t]he name being stolen from you will never change the facts appertaining to the case"…[and] the Legislature would have acted more consistently to have changed your name, as well as your town, to that of Atlanta.[184]

Atlanta Asides:

The first attempts to incorporate Atlanta as a city were met with protest. "Many of the citizens were decidedly hostile to the assumption of increased expenses and responsibilities attendant upon municipal incorporation."[185] There was a strong lobby in place which *helped defeat the measure* when it was brought before the Legislature in 1846.[186] The charter was ultimately granted though in 1847.[187] An early sign of the forward thinking of Atlanta's community leaders, a movement was started to have the State Capitol moved from Milledgeville to Atlanta *even before the charter was granted*.[188] The Capitol remained in Milledgeville though for another twenty years.[189]

There were several degraded parts of town in 1848. One was Murrel's Row which was located in the block between Decatur Street and Pryor Street.[190] Murrel's Row was named after John A. Murrel who was a famous Tennessee outlaw and was renowned for cock-fighting.[191] Another "tenderloin" district was known as "Snake Nation," now the name of the somewhat less rowdy younger-members guild of the Atlanta History Center.[192] Snake Nation, the tenderloin district, not the younger-members guild, was "devoted almost entirely to the criminal and immoral element."[193] It was located along what is now Peters Street from the railroad crossing to approximately the current intersection with Fair Street.[194]

Prior to 1850, the cemetery for Atlanta was located on the west side of Peachtree Street from Harris Street to beyond Baker Street and ran almost back to Williams Street.[195] It included the site on which the downtown Capitol City Club is located.

Map of area encompassing the former Atlanta Cemetery.

The cemetery was considered remote during the 1840's but it soon became clear that the city was growing in that direction.[196] In June of 1850, a six acre tract located at the present southwest corner of what is now Oakland cemetery was acquired for $75.00 per acre and the bodies interred at the Peachtree Street location were moved to the Oakland cemetery.[197] From 1850 to 1876, the cemetery was known as the Atlanta or City Cemetery.[198]

Dr. Crawford W. Long (1815-1878) was "the first person to successfully make use of anesthesia in a surgical operation."[199] Several years prior to 1850, he resided in Jefferson, Georgia where he practiced medicine and discovered anesthesia.[200] In 1850, he moved to Atlanta with his wife and two young daughters in order to grow his practice. After only one year, he determined that culturally Atlanta was not the best place to raise his daughters and moved the family to Athens.[201] Crawford Long Hospital in Atlanta is named after Dr. Long.

The Origin and Naming of Fulton County:

By 1853, the population of the city of Atlanta had reached 6,000 which far exceeded the population of Decatur which was then the county seat of DeKalb County.[202] Many Atlantans thought a new county should be created with Atlanta as the county seat.[203] A bill was introduced in the State Senate to "lay out and organize a new county from the county of DeKalb, and for other purposes," but the name of the new county was left blank.[204] Fulton County was thus carved out of DeKalb County. Upon a motion by John Collier, Senator from DeKalb, the bill was amended to insert the word "Fulton."[205]

The *Times and Sentinel*, of Columbus, Georgia reported the Senate action and stated that the new county was named in honor of Robert Fulton, the inventor of the steamboat.[206] Garrett writes that considerable discussion has taken place as to whether it was truly named in honor of Robert Fulton or whether it was in fact named after Hamilton Fulton, the civil engineer and surveyor referenced previously in the section entitled "The Georgia Canal Prospect."[207] Garrett submits that the discussion persisted because no historian could find or took the time to cite evidence on the subject and Hamilton Fulton seemed a more logical candidate for the honor.[208] As referenced previously in this book, the purpose of Hamilton Fulton's survey was to determine a route for either a canal or a railroad from the Tennessee

River to the Chattahoochee and to determine which was more feasible.[209] When the W & A route was surveyed 11 years later, the route followed substantially the survey laid out by Mr. Fulton.[210]

Robert Fulton, the inventor of the steamboat, was "never identified specifically with the State of Georgia by residence or activity."[211] He acquired national fame when on August 17, 1807, he piloted his steamboat, the Clermont, along the Hudson from New York City to Albany in 32 hours.[212] Garrett states that the steamboat did have a connection to Georgia since on May 26, 1819, the first steamship to cross the Atlantic, the Savannah, embarked from the port of Savannah.[213] As an aside, the Savannah was also equipped with sails and the crossing took 25 days.[214] A certain Dr. Angier was credited with suggesting the name "Fulton" for the new county and Garrett writes that he was from New Hampshire, came to Georgia long after Hamilton Fulton's day and probably did not know of Hamilton Fulton's works.[215] Garrett is forced to reluctantly conclude, even though he would have liked to have proved otherwise, that Fulton County was, in fact, named after Robert Fulton.[216]

The Not So Great:

Atlanta played a dubious role in the events leading up to the Civil War even before its strategic role during the War. During 1856, the "Kansas Question" or Freesoil movement was in full swing.[217] At that time, parties of Southern emigrants frequently and constantly passed through Atlanta to Kansas to turn the political scale there in favor of slavery.[218] "Large crowds would meet these Kansas emigrants at the depot to cheer them on, and often

31

to contribute to their necessities."[219] Further, "[b]oisterous Kansas meetings, addressed by fervid and fire-eating orators were of almost nightly occurrence in Atlanta during that summer."[220] Georgia was expected to "look after three of the thirty counties of Kansas territory, her sister Southern states taking care of three counties each."[221]

Should She Stay or Should She Go:

It is worth examining the events that led to Georgia's secession from the Union. It is often assumed that the decisions of Confederate States to secede from the Union reflected the unanimous consent of their citizens. It is interesting to note that the decision for Georgia to secede was not unanimous by any means. On January 2, 1861, an election was held in Fulton County to elect delegates to the January 16 convention in Milledgeville which was being convened to determine if Georgia should secede from the Union.[222] The Fulton delegation was pledged to vote for secession.[223] A majority of votes in DeKalb County, however, favored further efforts toward a peaceful resolution prior to secession. The ordinance in favor of secession was, of course, ultimately adopted and passed, but it was by no means unanimous, the vote tally being 208 in favor to 89 opposed.[224] Shortly thereafter, Atlanta actually made a bid to become the capital of the Confederacy. This was even before it was made the state capital of Georgia.[225]

The Confederate Commissary:

The only building in Atlanta erected by the Confederate government was the Confederate Commissary.[226] In late 1861, the Confederate government was looking for a central location to erect a building for the

Commissary Department.[227]   They chose the lot on which the Candler Building now stands.[228]

The owner demanded payment in gold, rejecting the payment in Confederate bonds that were offered.[229] The Confederate government ended up confiscating the land and building a two story frame building on the property. This building was seized by the Federal government and given to the Freedmen's Bureau.[230] The building was then actually put on rollers and moved to the northwest corner of Houston Street and Piedmont Avenue where it was eventually torn down in 1923.[231]

The Candler building now stands on the site of the former Confederate Commissary, the only building constructed by the Confederacy in Atlanta.

The Great Locomotive Heist:

One of the most fabled episodes of the Civil War originated in Kennesaw, Georgia. The famous commandeering of the "General" locomotive was intended to ensure the success of the Federal occupation of Chattanooga by General O. M. Mitchel.[232] The capture of the General was designed to sever the Western and Atlantic Railroad between Chattanooga and Atlanta by destroying the rails and bridges along the route between the two cities.[233]

There were twenty-two Federal raiders involved in the heist. They were made up of twenty Ohio soldiers and two Kentucky civilians, with James J. Andrews chosen to lead the mission.[234] They rendezvoused in Marietta, Georgia, spending the night of April 11, 1862 in various hotels in Marietta.[235] The next morning, twenty of the twenty-two men purchased tickets for various points along the W & A.[236] Among the group were locomotive engineers and firemen.[237] Two of the men, however, overslept and were left behind.[238]

Kennesaw Mountain, then called "Big Shanty", was chosen as the station where the train would be stolen because it did not have a telegraph office.[239] As planned, the train stopped at Big Shanty for its pre-scheduled 20 minute breakfast stop and all personnel and passengers departed the train leaving it completed unguarded.[240] Like clockwork, the raiders stole the train after everyone had disembarked.

The initial pursuit of the train was on foot, the pursuers believing that the train had been stolen by Confederate deserters and would be abandoned shortly up the tracks.[241] The mode of transport used in the second stage of the pursuit was not much faster. Two miles up the track, the pursuers came across a section foreman who offered his push car, "a vehicle propelled by poles in the hands of riders."[242]

The raid had been originally planned for April 11th, but Mr. Andrews postponed it to the 12th for reasons not elaborated on by Garrett. This postponement presented two problems for the raiders. The 11th was clear and dry, but the 12th was wet and "not conducive to bridge burning."[243] Additionally, southbound traffic on the railroad on the 11th was considerably lighter than on the 12th, an obvious hindrance if one is trying to travel north on the same line.[244] Chattanooga was in imminent danger from Federal troops at this time and was sending supplies and equipment south out of the city on the 12th.[245] Mr. Andrews, having a "suave manner," was able to "bluff his way past switch-tenders and station agents."[246] Notwithstanding that, at Kingston, Georgia, the raiders met their first serious delay when they were forced to wait for several southbound trains to pass.[247]

At the Etowah River, the pursuers ditched their pushcart and commandeered the locomotive "Yonah" which the raiders failed to decommission, "a fatal error" on their part.[248] The pursuers were also delayed at Kingston, Georgia, so they ditched the Yonah and commandeered the locomotive "William R. Smith" which was north of the congestion.[249] They were stopped in their tracks though in Adairsville, Georgia, where the raiders had destroyed the rails.[250] Two of the pursuers then ran for two miles up the tracks and flagged down the locomotive "Texas" which was heading southbound. The engineer of the Texas put the locomotive in reverse and continued the pursuit northbound.[251] They encountered two boxcars decoupled from the General which were left as obstacles on the tracks.[252] But the pursuers recoupled them (onto the back of the Texas, which, again, was running in reverse) and pushed them forward until they could be pushed off onto a spur.[253]

The General ran out of wood and water two miles above Ringgold, Georgia, and the raiders took to the woods.[254] All of the raiders were rounded up almost immediately and jailed in Chattanooga.[255] They were sentenced to be hanged on June 7th and 18th in Chattanooga, but the movements of the Federal troops caused the executions to be moved to Atlanta.[256]

Mr. Andrews managed to escape on June 2, but was recaptured the next day.[257] Mr. Andrews and eight of the raiders were put to death near the present intersection of Juniper and Third Street, but eight of the raiders escaped from Fulton County jail on October 16, 1862, and made their way behind Union lines.[258] The remaining men were traded as prisoners of war.[259] The General now sits as a permanent exhibit at the Kennesaw Civil War Museum.

Battle of Kennesaw Mountain:

The battle of Kennesaw Mountain was almost avoided by Sherman, but weather and the political season made him decide otherwise. Sherman apparently had the option of avoiding a frontal assault on the heavily armed positions on Kennesaw by attempting a flanking movement, but muddy roads from a rainy June made that particularly difficult.[260] Additionally, "the troops were tired of marching and wanted to fight."[261] Perhaps most significantly, President Lincoln was up for re-election and needed a victory to bolster his policy of continuing the war.[262] Sherman believed that if successful, "all military resistance in north Georgia might be ended; if it failed, the flanking movement still could be attempted."[263]

Sherman made the assault at two separate points, one south of Kennesaw Mountain along Burnt Hickory Road and the other at a point south of Dallas Road defended by General Cheatham (now known as Cheatham's Hill).[264] Sherman assaulted Cheatham's Hill with 8,000 troops and directed 5,500 troops on the point south of Kennesaw.[265] Sherman lost 1,580 men versus 200 Confederates killed at Cheatham's Hill and 600 men versus 300 Confederates at the point south of Kennesaw, such that the attack was a failure for Sherman.[266] A large number of Federal troops killed at Kennesaw were actually buried in the National Cemetery in Marietta.[267]

Cheatham's Hill at Kennesaw Mountain, one of two major points of attack by the Federal army in The Battle of Kennesaw Mountain.

National Cemetery in Marietta, Georgia where a large number of Federal troops killed in the Battle of Kennesaw Mountain are buried.

With this defeat and realizing that Kennesaw could only be taken with extreme casualties, Sherman resumed his flanking movements and in reaction, on the night of July 2, the Confederates withdrew from Kennesaw Mountain.[268]

Sherman Advances:

Sherman decided against a frontal assault upon General Johnston's fortified line and decided to cross the Chattahoochee at various points from Pace's Ferry to Roswell, Georgia.[269] The crossing of the first unit resulted in an interesting story. The first unit to cross the Chattahoochee was the 23rd Corps of the Army of the Ohio, commanded by Major-General John M. Schofield on the afternoon of July 8, 1864.[270] The unit crossed practically unopposed at the mouth of Soap Creek at Isom's Ferry about equidistant between Powers Ferry and Johnston's Ferry.

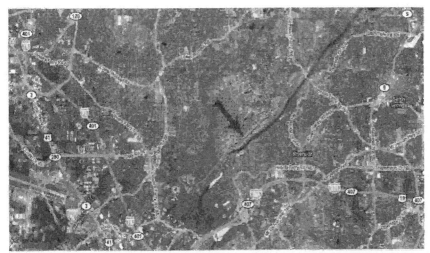

The arrow indicates the location of Soap Creek on the Chattahoochee. Although difficult to read, the road crossing the Chattahoochee River to the north is Johnson's Ferry Road.

"The crossing came as a complete surprise to a Confederate outpost upon a ridge on the Fulton County side of the river."[271]   Garrett quotes (Federal) General Jacob D. Cox's account of the event as follows:

> **In the deserted camp of the outpost, in which even the half-cooked supper was left, an unfinished letter from one of the Confederate soldiers to his wife was found. In it he calms her fears for his safety, saying that he is now almost as free from peril as if he were at home on his plantation.[272]**

One can only imagine the surprise of this Confederate soldier believing he is miles from the front, daydreaming of the plantation and Mr. Bluebird on his shoulder, and then, out of the blue, there's the 23rd Corps of the Union Army crossing the river right in front of him. General Johnston crossed the Chattahoochee to the Fulton County side on pontoons near the Western & Atlantic Railroad Bridge on the night of July 9, 1884.[273] General

Johnston then set up his headquarters in a house located at what is now known as 1030-1034 West Marietta Street.[274] It took until July 17, 1864, for Sherman to have all of his armies across the river and ready for the advance on Atlanta.[275]

The Replacement of General Johnston With General Hood:

It is common knowledge that on July 17th, General Johnston, who was charged with defending Atlanta, received the telegraph relieving him of command of the Army of Tennessee and transferring command to a new general, General Hood.[276] Garrett expounds upon the personality conflicts giving rise to the move and promotes the generally held view that it was not a strategically sound move. Garrett writes that a "mutual distrust" existed between General Johnston and Confederate President Davis and Chief-of-Staff Braxton Bragg.[277] General Johnston's policy of strategic withdrawal was viewed as "evidence of military incompetence [and the] fact that Johnston was outnumbered about two to one, seemed not to enter, with much weight at least, into their calculations."[278] There were even some questionable actions taken by General Hood, who, at the time of the change in command, was commanding a corps in General Johnston's army. Apparently General Hood wrote a letter to Chief-of-Staff Bragg charging General Johnston with incompetency.[279]

Garrett writes that the removal of General Johnston was unfortunate for both General Johnston and the Southern cause.[280] He further asserts that "[i]t is certain that the change of Confederate commanders was learned with satisfaction by every officer and man in the Federal army...[since t]he patient skill and watchful intelligence and courage with which Johnston had always confronted them with impregnable fortifications, had been exasperating."[281] According to Garrett, most of the Army of the Tennessee were shocked and unpleasantly surprised by the change in command.[282] "Hood was simply not popular with the majority of his subordinate officers and was looked upon with some distrust by the rank and file."[283]

Sherman as Houseguest:

Apparently Sherman, though not so trustworthy with a book of matches, was overall a pretty considerate houseguest. During his time in the Atlanta area, he stayed in several different residences, the owners of which had evidently vacated to safer locales. Sherman spent the night of July 18, 1864, at the brick house which is still standing and is now the Peachtree Golf Club Clubhouse.[284] The house and surrounding property were owned at the time by Samuel House (1798-1873) who was a native of South Carolina.[285] The bricks of the house were actually made on the property.[286]

Photograph of the Peachtree Golf Club clubhouse on Ashford Dunwoody Road where Sherman spent the night of July 18, 1864.

Sherman spent the night of July 19, 1864 at the James Oliver Powell house which was situated on the west side of Clairmont Road between North Decatur Road and Peachtree Creek.[287] The following day he moved his headquarters to a tent at the northwest intersection of North Decatur and Briarcliff Road, which was called Williams Mill Road at the time.[288]

By September 7, Sherman had established his headquarters in Atlanta in one of the "newest and finest" homes in Atlanta.[289] It was owned by John Neal and located at the southwest corner of Washington and Mitchell Streets.[290] Remarkably, Sherman left the house in "excellent condition, and the Neal furniture, stored in the parlor, was disturbed but little."[291] After the war, the Neal House was used as a hotel for several years. In 1870, it became the first home of Oglethorpe College and was then used to house the Atlanta Girls High School. It was ultimately torn down in 1928 to make way for the new City Hall which was completed in 1930.[292]

The Battle of Peachtree Creek:

General Hood was attentive to the (Federal) Army of the Cumberland's movement at Peachtree Creek in what is now the Buckhead area of Atlanta. His strategy was to attack and overwhelm (Federal) General Thomas' units as they crossed Peachtree Creek as they were "widely separated from the left of Sherman's long line."[293] He had also been ordered by the authorities in Richmond to turn back the Federals before they reached Atlanta.[294] Atlanta did not extend that far north at that time.

The ensuing conflict was known as the Battle of Peachtree Creek. The first attack was originally scheduled for noon on July 20, 1864, but it was delayed until 4:30 p.m. and by that time, according to Garrett, General Thomas was ready.[295] Among the divisions sent forth from the outer defense line of the city were divisions commanded by Loring and Walthall.[296] Walthall advanced along Howell Mill Road and Loring from the high hill which is now Loring Heights neighborhood.[297] Garrett describes the events as follows:

> **Loring struck Benjamin Harrison's brigade at Collier's Mill, and Geary's division between the mill and the present course of Northside Drive. Walthall's men surged across the Hiram Embry farm, where Collier Road joins Howell Mill Road, and rushed Williams' division of the 20th corps posted behind a deep ravine at what is now Norfleet Road. It was a gallant attack, delivered with spirit, and it nearly succeeded at Northside Drive where Walthall's men penetrated a gap between Geary's refused right and the left of Williams behind the ravine above mentioned. Indeed, this ravine had so distorted the Federal alignment that only the stubborn rally of Geary's regiments around his artillery on Collier Road saved the day. A storm center of the Confederate attack was at Collier's Mill, where the road crosses Tanyard branch. Here the 27th Alabama captured the state flag of the 33rd New Jersey, but everywhere along the line the men in gray were repulsed, and darkness closed down a bloody field, still held by the bluecoats."[298]

There were 1,710 Union casualties and 4,796 Confederate casualties at the Battle of Peachtree Creek, described by Garrett as "a bad start for Hood in the defense of Atlanta."[299]

There is a monument commemorating the Battle of Peachtree Creek erected on Peachtree Road across from Brighton Road (in front of Piedmont Hospital) which marks the approximate location of the commencement of the Battle of Peachtree Creek.[300]

Photograph of monument commemorating the Battle of Peachtree Creek, monument is located in front of Piedmont Hospital on Peachtree Road.

The Loss of Confederate General Walker:

General Hood withdrew all his troops from the outer line to the Atlanta fortifications before dawn of July 22, 1864.[301] "The march began about dark of the 21st from the present intersection of Spring and Peachtree streets and proceeded down Peachtree to Five Points."[302] General Hood wanted General Hardee's corps to get around the rear of (Federal) General McPherson's army in East Atlanta and then simultaneously send General Cheatham's corps to assault the Federal front.[303]

General Hood had planned for General Hardee to attack the Federals in East Atlanta at daybreak.[304] General Hardee, however, had no maps and "the country was thoroughly unfamiliar to them."[305] By daybreak General Hardee had only reached a point along what is now Bouldercrest Drive due to "trying marching conditions and the fatigue of the soldiery."[306] General Walker, one of General Hardee's generals, proceeded toward Decatur along the Fayetteville Road.[307]

Garrett writes that "[h]ad General Walker obeyed Hood's instructions, he would have kept on the Fayetteville Road nearly to Decatur before turning westward."[308] But he did not, and it cost him his life. General Walker detoured to the left at Sugar Creek and ran into a mill pond which he was then forced to detour around.[309] Once arriving at the present Glenwood Avenue, he swung around to a point approximately where Wilkinson Drive joins Glenwood.[310] Here General Walker was shot off his horse and killed instantly by a Federal picket as he surveyed the area with his binoculars.[311]

A monument was erected to honor Confederate General Walker 1/5th mile west of Sugar Creek on Glenwood Avenue, July 22, 1902, on the 38th anniversary of the battle.[312] In 1930, research was conducted however, which tended to show he was killed to the east of Sugar Creek and as a result, the monument was moved to Wilkinson Drive and Glenwood Avenue in August, 1936.[313]

Photograph of monument located at present day intersection of Wilkinson Drive and Glenwood Avenue where Confederate General Walker was shot due in part to a wrong turn.

Combat in Decatur:

There was actually hand-to-hand combat in and around the Court House Square in Decatur.[314] General Wheeler drove Schofield's 23rd (Federal) corps in hand-to-hand fighting from Decatur.[315] But General Wheeler was called to aid General Hardee who was nearby and had to retire from the town and give up the gains accomplished there.[316]

The Shelling of Atlanta:

It is almost impossible to imagine that Atlanta was shelled just like Sarajevo or other war-torn cities but to a lesser degree, it happened. The first shell fired by the Federals fell at the corner of Ellis and Ivy Streets on

46

Wednesday, July 20, 1864, the day of the Battle of Peachtree Creek and resulted in the death of a small child.[317] From July 20th to August 9th, 1864, the city was subject to light shelling "during which period the citizens went about their daily affairs with little precaution against the ever present danger, though the prudent kept away from the railroads, church spires and tall chimneys."[318]

Most of the shells were launched from Federal corps batteries "along what is now 8th Street, N.W. on high ground near Howell Mill Road, and from the 16th corps guns on an elevation...[near] Simpson Street west of Ashley."[319]

One victim of the shelling, an African-American man who was a barber, was hit by a fragment that struck a lamppost, ricocheted and then exploded while he was standing on the corner of Whitehall and Alabama Streets.[320] The lamppost was kept in City Hall until 1880 as a symbol of the War. In 1880, it was restored to its original site at the northeast corner of Whitehall and Alabama Streets. In December, 1939, in preparation for the world premier of *Gone With The Wind*, it was again lighted with gas.[321] Now it resides at Underground Atlanta.

Photograph of Civil War lamppost hit by Union shelling during shelling of Atlanta and kept as a symbol of the War. Crack in iron base from impact still visible.

During the shelling, General Hood wrote several letters to Sherman regarding the bombardment stating it was "unwarranted by the usages of civilized warfare and barbarous in the extreme."[322] Sherman was apparently not persuaded.

The Surrender of Atlanta:

General Hood realized by September 1, 1864, that Atlanta could no longer be held and began making preparations to evacuate the city.[323] By midnight on September 1, most of the Confederate troops had left the city.[324] On the evening of the withdrawal, General Hood ordered his men to set flame to his ammunition trains, seven locomotives and 81 loaded cars.[325] Garrett describes the state of affairs on September 2, 1864 "when Atlanta, worn out and shattered by the storm of war, lay stranded between two flags, under the protection of neither, abandoned by one, and with little hope of mercy from the other."[326]

The City was not formally surrendered by General Hood, so on September 2, 1864, Mayor James M. Calhoun decided to take care of this himself.[327] Mayor Calhoun and the group that accompanied him set out along Marietta Street to find the Federals. At a point where Curran Street originated at Marietta Street (near the present northwest corner of the Georgia Tech Campus), Mayor Calhoun came across a small body of Federal troops commanded by Captain H. M. Scott. A larger body of Federal troops then arrived and instructed Mayor Calhoun to write out his desire to surrender to Brigadier-General William T. Ward, the nearest general officer, which he did.[328] Federal troops began occupying Atlanta the same day (September 2, 1864).[329]

Remnants of the Occupation:

General George H. Thomas, who was appointed by Sherman to garrison Atlanta, chose to occupy a Greek Revival home on the west side of Peachtree Street between Ellis and Cain.[330] Designed by John Boutell, a pioneer Atlanta architect, and built in 1858 or 1859, it was ultimately torn down in February, 1913 by Asa G. Candler.[331] However, the columns which adorned the front and sides of the home were "removed to Woodberry School, 149 Peachtree Circle, in Ansley Park," which is now an apartment building.[332]

The Columns on this present day apartment building in Ansley Park were taken from a Greek Revival home on Peachtree where Federal General Thomas stayed during the occupation of Atlanta.

Forced to Leave:

Sherman issued Special Orders No. 67 on September 4th, 1864, which required that the city be vacated "by all except the armies of the United States, and such civilians as may be retained."[333] Accordingly, between September 9th and September 11th, 705 adults and 860 children were removed from the city.[334]

Sherman Leaves Atlanta on His March to the Sea:

Garrett writes that "[b]y November 8th, Sherman's plans for the evacuation of Atlanta and the march to the sea had been formulated."[335] On November 12, Sherman ordered the railroad and telegraph lines to Tennessee and North Georgia cut and the W. & A. Railroad Bridge over the Chattahoochee burned.[336] The Federal army bound for Savannah consisted of "62,204 officers and men, including, besides infantry, 5,063 cavalry and 1,812 artillery."[337]

With regard to the burning of Atlanta, Garrett writes that "Sherman's primary objective insofar as the destruction of Atlanta was concerned can be classified as military…[t]herefore the Federal commander determined to make Atlanta not only untenable militarily and industrially but to render it useless as a future base for Confederate operations."[338] He thus ordered the destruction of "industrial and railroad plant, public buildings and warehouses."[339] The intent was apparently not to burn down the entire city.

There is an interesting story behind the reprieve of several institutions. The Medical College was saved from Sherman's destruction through the clever actions of Dr. P. Noel D'Alvigny, a faculty member. He gained the assistance of his hospital attendants by giving them all whisky and convincing them to act sick and wounded. He showed the Federal officer the carefully crafted scene and was given until daybreak to get the building vacated, but "[b]y that time the Federal army was on the march and the danger was past."[340] The Masonic Hall located on Decatur Street at the time was saved due to the influence of the local members with brother members in the Federal army.[341]

It did not take long, however, for Atlanta to start rebuilding. Garrett writes that by December 15th, many of the citizens were starting to return and rebuild.[342]

Years after the War, General Sherman returned to Atlanta with his two daughters and several aides for a tour on January 29, 1879.[343] Quoting a diary of a contemporary city resident, Garrett writes that "there was no perceptible indignation or feeling of prejudice."[344]

The Reconstruction Era:

During the early part of President Johnson's administration (1865-1869), it appeared that it would be a peaceful reconstruction.[345] The Federal appointments "gave considerable satisfaction to the people of Atlanta."[346] Garrett writes that during 1866, the government of Georgia "functioned normally except for the presence of Federal troops and the Freedmen's Bureau."[347] But in Washington, 1866 marked the beginning of the struggle between the President and the Congress over the execution of the reconstruction.[348] President Johnson's plan followed the logic of President Lincoln, that the Southern States had never seceded from the Union, but that their attempt to do so "placed them in a condition of suspended vitality."[349] The President appealed to the nation in the congressional election of 1866, but radicals carried both houses of Congress by sweeping majorities, thereby eliminating the possibility for President Johnson's program of reconstruction.[350]

The Streetcar:

The plan for a streetcar system for Atlanta was conceived in 1866. The Atlanta Street Railroad Company was incorporated by an Act of the Legislature on February 23, 1866.[351] Later that year, the incorporators received a franchise from the City of Atlanta to construct streetcar tracks on certain streets, but "the franchise contained so many burdensome restrictions in the way of paving requirements and otherwise that the company was unable to proceed under it, and the population of Atlanta continued to walk."[352]

Baseball in Atlanta:

Garrett writes that "[n]early thirty years after its first introduction at Cooperstown, New York, baseball came to Atlanta in the spring of 1866."[353] A certain Captain Tom Burnett organized "The Atlanta Baseball Club."[354] According to Garrett, "[t]he players were as green as the grass upon which they played."[355] Shortly after the inception of The Atlanta Baseball Club, a rival team was organized known as "The Gate City Nine."[356] In their inaugural game in 1866, the ball was not pitched, but "tossed out with careless grace."[357] Accordingly, the score ended up 127 to 29 in favor of the Gate City Nine Club.[358] Subsequently, in 1872, another baseball club was introduced called the "Osceolas."[359] The catcher was Charlie Pemberton, the son of John S. Pemberton who later became the creator of Coca-Cola.[360]

Were You Aware:

Samuel Walker was born in Georgia in 1791 and came to Fulton County in the 1820's. He formed and operated a mill on Clear Creek "at about the point where a bridge over that stream and the Southern Railway belt line connects Piedmont Park with Boulevard Park [now known as Virginia Highlands]."[361]

Map showing approximate location of Samuel Walker's mill.

One of his children, Benjamin F. Walker, sold the property in 1887, to the Gentlemen's Driving Club, predecessor to the Piedmont Driving Club, a prominent social club in midtown Atlanta.[362] One of the millstones of Samuel Walker's mill adorns the Piedmont Driving Club.[363]

A vein of gold was discovered on Nancy Creek near the Chattahoochee River in 1866.[364] Garrett describes the area as near Randall Mill Road and Mount Paran Road, neither of which were in existence at the time.

This map shows the intersection of Mt. Paran Road and Randall Mill Road, where gold was once discovered.

No one got rich off the discovery though as the "quality and quantity were too meager to warrant extensive mining efforts."[365]

Downtown Atlanta almost had its own Park Avenue. In 1875, there was a movement to rename Pryor Street as Park Avenue.[366] It was opposed by a number of citizens including a prominent friend of Allen W. Pryor after whom the street was named, and the change did not occur.[367] There is a Park Place in downtown Atlanta, but it was not connected to the proposed renaming of Pryor Street.

The Old Fourth Ward:

The term "Old Fourth Ward" has survived all these years and is still used to describe the area comprising the Fourth Ward of Atlanta. The areas making up the other four wards have not retained their "Ward designation" as their primary identification in common real estate parlance. There were four other wards which were laid out as follows:

> **First Ward:** --On North by W & A R R, East by Whitehall Street, and on the South and West by corporate line.

> **Second Ward:** --On North by W & A and Ga Rail Road, East by Calhoun and McDonough Streets, West by Whitehall Street, and South by corporate line.

> **Third Ward:** --On North by Ga R R, West by Calhoun and McDonough Streets, and on the South and East by corporate line.

> **Fourth Ward:** --On South by Ga R R, West by Ivy Street, and on the North and East by corporate line.

> **Fifth Ward:** --On South by W & A R R, East by Ivy Street, and on the North and West by corporate line.[368]

Post-Civil War Atlanta Firsts:

The first lottery was authorized in late 1866, when the Legislature passed "[a]n Act to so far modify the laws against lotteries as to enable [certain individuals]…to adopt a scheme to raise money for the purpose of building a home for and supporting indigent widows and orphans."[369] It was called The Georgia State Lottery.[370] Interestingly enough, the orphans' home was never built and the funds were used instead to aid "the cause of education."[371] Later, on February 24, 1877, the Legislature passed an act "making lotteries illegal, and repealing all conflicting laws."[372] Garrett explains that "with better times and the end of reconstruction, the need for legalized lotteries had passed."[373]

The first roller-skating rink was opened in Atlanta in 1870, on Forsyth Street.[374] Garrett writes that a "great walking craze" took hold of the city in 1871, with matches held in the roller skating rink on Forsyth.[375] One such match lasted twenty hours.[376] The roller-skating rink declined in popularity however when a young woman was fatally injured from a roller-skating accident there.[377]

The first air-brakes were placed on the W. & A. locomotives during 1871.[378] Before the invention of the air-brake by George Westinghouse in 1869, "stopping a train, especially on a down grade, was hazardous and uncertain."[379] Garrett writes "[w]ith only a hand brake on the locomotive, the engineer had little control of his train, and in an emergency, could only blow for brakes and hope that the brakemen could set the hand brakes on the individuals cars in time to avert an accident."[380]

The first casualty of the Atlanta volunteer fire department occurred on March 23, 1871, but was not caused by fighting an actual fire.[381] Dan Lynch, foreman of Tallulah Company No. 3, was the victim. Mr. Lynch's engine house was equipped with a "hand engine" pulled by men rather than by horse or mule.[382] On route to a fire the evening of the 23rd, Mr. Lynch, who was pulling the hand engine, fell to the street from exhaustion caused from fighting a previous fire that day. When he fell, he was run over by the engine and died within 15 minutes.[383] Garrett writes that "by 1875, horses had come into general use by the fire department, which saved the volunteer members thereof the physical strain and danger of pulling the equipment."[384]

The Atlanta public school system was opened in 1872.[385] The election of a board of education had occurred in late 1869 and an Act of Legislature on September 30, 1870 "had empowered the Mayor and Council of Atlanta to establish and maintain a system of Public Schools within the city."[386] The Atlanta schools were originally organized as grammar and high schools only.[387] Grammar school ran from age 6 through age 14 and high school ran from age 14 through age 18.[388]

The Atlanta police department up until 1873 had been mainly comprised of a marshal and deputies of varying numbers.[389] Garrett writes that this gave way in 1873 "to a regularly constituted uniformed police force, headed by a chief and governed by a board of police commissioners."[390] The uniform was a "tin-helmet, Prince-Albert coat uniform."[391] Up until the uniformed police force was organized, it was the custom for the marshals on patrol to call the hours of the night, e.g., "twelve o'clock and all's well."[392]

Residents of Atlanta relied on wells, pumps and cisterns for water until the fall of 1875 when the first *public waterworks system* was completed.[393]

Atlanta's infamous traffic apparently became a problem as early as 1877, though the penalties for a moving violation were stiffer than today. On March 5, 1877, a traffic ordinance was passed "which prohibited driving more than five unhaltered mules between 8:30 a.m. and 5:30 p.m."[394] Violators could be fined up to $100.00 and/or a month in prison.[395]

Use of the telephone began in Atlanta in 1877, one year after its invention by Alexander Graham Bell.[396] The Western & Atlantic Railroad was the first user of the new technology, linking up its passenger agents' office and the Union Station.[397] By 1879, Atlanta had 55 subscribers to telephone service. In 1884, "Long Distance" meant calling to Decatur, that being the terminus of the sole long distance circuit in Atlanta at the time.[398] The long distance charges were 15 cents per five minutes.[399] The original telephone operators were boys, but they apparently had a tendency to "talk back to subscribers in rough and ready language" such that they were replaced by women operators in 1888.

The Rise of Rich's Department Store (Now Macy's):

Morris Rich (1847-1928) was a native of Kashau, Hungary and came to America at the age of 13 "penniless and almost without education."[400] His first regular job was that of "a clerk in a small mercantile store in Cleveland, Ohio."[401] By the age of 18, he had started small stores in Chattanooga, Tennessee and then later in Albany, Georgia.[402] His brother, William, meanwhile had started a dry goods business in Atlanta known as William Rich & Company.[403] In May of 1867, Morris borrowed $1,000.00 from his brother and rented a little store at 36 Whitehall Street. Mr. Rich started his business "in an era of barter and trade…but he firmly set forth the fact that his goods had one price to all, based on value and a proper margin of profit."[404] William, Morris and a third brother joined forces in 1876, and in

1881, opened M. Rich and Brothers, a new store, at 54-56 Whitehall Street.[405] This store had the first plate-glass show windows in Atlanta which was a significant and daring marketing move since typically, show windows of the day were small and closed at night due to vandalism.[406] In 1901, a six story annex was added with elevator service and the store was "departmentalized" into a department store.[407]

Garrett writes that "[t]his last innovation brought forth heated complaint from numerous customers, accustomed through the years to being waited upon by their favorite clerk in any part of the store...[but] it was patiently explained that the more specialized service would redound to the benefit of customers, and in time the innovation was accepted."[408] In the spring of 1924, the store moved to the nucleus of its final location at Broad and Alabama Streets.[409] Rich's was ultimately sold to Federated Department Stores (now known as Macy's, Inc.). The building now houses the Sam Nunn Atlanta Federal Center.

Former Rich's Department Store in downtown Atlanta, now the Sam Nunn Atlanta Federal Center.

Atlanta Becomes the Capital City:

In December, 1868, as part of the Reconstruction, a Constitutional Convention was called by military order and held under military supervision in Atlanta.[410] The Constitution of 1868 was very progressive in many ways, providing for mechanics liens (which allow subcontractors and suppliers of materials to lien an owner's property if they are not paid), a prohibition on dueling and a direction to the General Assembly to provide a thorough system of general free education to all the children of the State.[411] It also progressed the stature and growth of the City of Atlanta. "On February 26, 1868, a special meeting of City Council was called to make a formal proposal to the Constitutional Convention of what the city would do, provided the removal of the State Capital from Milledgeville to Atlanta was incorporated into the Constitution.[412] The incentives must have been sweet enough, as the relocation of the Capitol to Atlanta was included in the Constitution.

The Atlanta Constitution:

The *Atlanta Constitution*, now the *Atlanta Journal & Constitution*, was established by Colonel Carey W. Styles, a veteran of two wars (Mexican War and Civil War), a lawyer by profession and the former mayor of Brunswick, where he had "killed a man under justified circumstances."[413] Garrett describes the origin of the name of the paper as follows:

> **Styles obtained the idea for the paper's name from President Andrew Johnson. Styles made a trip to New York in May to purchase type and materials and on his way back to Atlanta he stopped in Washington to congratulate the President on the**

failure of the recent impeachment proceedings against him. Johnson recalled that before the war there had been a democratic daily in Washington called *The Constitution*. He suggested the appropriateness of the name to Styles, who liked the idea and christened his new paper accordingly.[414]

A State - Yet Not a State:

The Georgia Legislature voted against the ratification of the 15th Amendment in March, 1869.[415] In response, Congress then remanded the state to military jurisdiction with the added requirement that the Fifteenth Amendment be ratified as a condition of readmission to the Union.[416] Garrett points out an interesting fact about the passage of the 14th and 15th Amendments, which of course, required the ratification by three-fourths of the states for passage. Garrett writes:

> [t]he validity of the Fourteenth Amendment was partially resting on Georgia's ratification as a state, and yet [at the time of ratification] she was not a State, though the ratification was claimed as valid. The State was not allowed to be a State, and yet its ratification of the Fifteenth Amendment was sought; the act of a State, before it should become a State.[417]

Air Travel in Atlanta:

Atlanta's first experience with aviation did not involve the airplane. On December 10, 1869, a dentist by the name of Dr. Albert Hape and a certain Professor Samuel A. King launched Mr. King's hot air balloon, named Hyperion.[418] The launch site was in the vicinity of Marietta and

Walton Streets and it drew a large crowd.[419] *The Constitution* reported that it probably reached an altitude of one mile.[420] The Hyperion landed after a successful flight six miles north of Alpharetta, Georgia.[421]

Another flight was planned for New Year's Day in 1870, and it drew an even larger crowd.[422] Mr. King, at the last minute, determined the balloon was unsafe, but Dr. Hape did not want to disappoint the crowd and ascended in the balloon without him.[423] According to the sources cited by Garrett, at an altitude of about a mile, the balloon exploded, but Dr. Hape somehow managed to survive and rode back into town on a horse about an hour later.[424] He had apparently miraculously parachuted to the ground using a large piece of canvas and landed unconscious near the Chattahoochee River about three miles out from town.[425] Dr. Hape's older brother, Samuel, also a dentist, some years later founded the town of Hapeville, which of course abuts the Hartsfield-Jackson Atlanta International Airport.

Mitchell Giveth and Mitchell's Heirs Taketh Away - (The Breakup of the State Square):

The City of Atlanta lost a good portion of its original downtown property including its original park under interesting circumstances. When Samuel Mitchell granted to the State of Georgia the five acres known as the State Square, it was subject to a right of reversion if the property was ever not used for railroad purposes.[426] In other words, title to the property would revert back to Samuel Mitchell or his heirs if the property was ever used for another purpose. According to Garrett, "[i]n 1846, he made a similarly restricted grant to the Macon and Western R.R. for the land between the W. & A. right-of-way and Alabama Street."[427] In 1853, "the freight house, shops and offices of the W. & A. that had been built there were removed and a few years later the City of Atlanta was granted the right by the State to create a park between the depot and Decatur Street."[428] As a precaution, the City ran a side track into this area to try and prevent reversion of the property.[429] The Macon and Western Railroad was removed in 1865, and in 1867, the heirs of Samuel Mitchell filed suit to recover all of the land since it was not being used for railroad purposes.[430]

A settlement was entered resulting in the State's keeping "the park property north of the depot with a space reserved for a street which was subsequently opened as Wall Street."[431] The State, in return, conveyed to the heirs the remainder of the tract, which was "for the most part south of the depot."[432] A portion of the property was then auctioned off, one portion being the lot at the northwest corner of Pryor and what was to become Wall Street which is how Atlanta lost its original park.[433]

Map with arrow indicating approximate location of area lost by Atlanta due to violation of original deed restriction.

Underground Atlanta and Knights in Shining Armor:

During the fall of 1870, the first of an annual series of Georgia State Fairs was held at the newly acquired Oglethorpe Park.[434] This park later became the Exposition Cotton Mills which was a manifestation of Atlanta's early marketing efforts and was used to attract new business to the City.

Location of Old Exposition Cotton Mills at 841 Ashby Street.

One feature of the new fair was a tournament in which competitors clad in full knight's armor, tried to catch on their lances the largest number of rings swung from a post.[435] The entrants from different parts of the state donned names such as the "Knight of Euharlee" and the "Knight of Oconee."[436]

This unique event ended in tragedy, however, when Michael E. Kenny, an Irish resident and owner of the Chicago Ale Depot on Pryor Street, was thrown against a post by his horse and killed.[437] Garrett states "Kenny's Alley, running east from Pryor to Central Avenue, bears the name of this popular citzen (sic)."[438] Now Kenny's Alley and Underground Atlanta appear to be following the fate of Michael Kenny, albeit a much slower and capital intensive demise.

Sculpture of Michael Kenney at Kenney's Alley in Underground Atlanta.

Present day Kenney's Alley at Underground Atlanta.

Oglethorpe University:

Oglethorpe University opened in January, 1838, in Midway, Georgia "near Milledgeville in Baldwin County under the auspices of the Presbyterian Church," but was shut down as a result of the Civil War.[439] Its endowment was lost in Confederate bonds. There were unsuccessful attempts to reopen at Midway after the War, but the relocation of the Capital from Milledgeville to Atlanta was what brought Oglethorpe back into existence.[440] When the Capitol was moved, the City of Atlanta pledged an endowment of $40,000.00 and in 1869, the trustees voted for the relocation.[441]

Interestingly enough, the Neal House (where Sherman stayed during the War) was purchased for the University and on October 4, 1870, the school was reopened. One of the initial faculty members, an Oglethorpe graduate, class of 1848, was Reverend Donald Fraser. An interesting historical link: Fritz Orr was a great grandson of Reverend Fraser, Fritz being the former owner of the Fritz Orr Camp which is now encompassed within the campus of The Westminster Schools.

Unfortunately, due to financial troubles, the University had to be closed, once again, in 1872.[442] The University was refounded and once again reopened its doors in 1916 and, of course, currently flourishes at its present site on Peachtree Road. Although Presbyterians contributed to the revival of the institution, it was re-established as a nondenominational independent university. One of Oglethorpe's most unique landmarks, Hermance Stadium, was originally intended to be a full, bowl-style stadium. However, its donor Harry Hermance dedicated the first section on October 26, 1929, then lost his entire fortune three days later.[443] The structure is only 1/8th of the originally planned structure and has never been completed.[444]

Photograph of Hermance Stadium at Oglethorpe University which to this day stands only 1/8th completed.

The Atlanta Streetcar: Take Two:

In the early 1870's, transportation within the city limits was becoming problematic since there was rapid expansion, most streets were unpaved and there were very few sidewalks.[445] Carriages frequently got bogged down on principal streets.[446] "[I]n 1872, the *Columbus Sun* referred to Atlanta as the 'Mud City.'"[447] This led promoters of a streetcar system to try again. The City Council in January, 1869, adopted a resolution repealing "the more objectionable features of the previous franchise" and exempting the rolling stock from taxation for a period of years."[448] One new requirement though, and one that continued through at least 1954, if not the end of the streetcar system in Atlanta, was that the streetcar company became responsible for paving between the tracks and for three feet on each side of the tracks.[449] The Council feared the pounding of the hooves of the horses pulling the streetcars would wear out the pavement.[450]

The passage of the resolution, however, did not lead to the immediate construction of a streetcar system.[451] Finally, on April 25, 1871, two Atlanta leading citizens, Richard Peters and George W. Adair, purchased the charter and franchise of the old company and organized the Atlanta Street Railway Company.[452] The first line was two miles long and was known as the West End line.[453] Garrett writes that it was probably not accidental that the line ran by Mr. Peters' home at Mitchell and Forsyth Streets and terminated near the residence of Mr. Adair in front of the McPherson Barracks.[454] The original track ran as follows: "[t]he cast iron rails began on Whitehall Street at the railroad crossing and extended out Whitehall to Mitchell, thence along Mitchell to Forsyth, out Forsyth to Peters, and along Peters Street to the Barracks."[455] To inspire confidence and peace of mind, the management of the company published notices such as the following:

> **The drivers of the streetcars are mostly married men, citizens of Atlanta, and are so careful of their duties that ladies by themselves could ride in perfect safety at any hour of the day from one end of the line to the other.[456]**

An interesting innovation, the toll box on each car had a clear glass top "so the driver could count his money and check on his passengers.[457]

Ponce de Leon and Atlanta's First Bottled Water:

There was an early "watering place" in the Atlanta area known as Yancey Spring.[458] It was located in the low ground south of the intersection of the Southern Railway belt line (f.k.a. Air-Line Railroad) and Ponce de Leon Avenue.[459]

Environmental protections were still a long way off and the Yancey Spring was apparently buried under a fill as part of the construction of the Air-Line Railroad in 1868.[460] A new source for drinking water had to be found for the railroad camp building the line, so a party from the camp was sent out to find a new source for drinking water. They located new springs where City Hall East now stands (formerly the Sears-Roebuck building).[461]

Photograph of City Hall East on Ponce de Leon Avenue, the former site of the Ponce de Leon Springs and Resort.

Map with arrow indicating approximate location of Ponce de Leon Springs.

There was a considerable amount of sickness among the men in the railroad camp, and according to Garrett's sources, the men who were sick found themselves getting steadily better after drinking the water from the two springs exclusively for a few weeks.[462] Word spread of the medicinal value of the springs, and Atlantans began to drive the two miles to the springs which "soon became a resort."[463] In 1870, the site became officially known as Ponce de Leon Springs, the name having been suggested by a former physician, Dr. Henry L. Wilson, "in recognition of the value of the water in giving renewed health and vitality to those who drink it regularly."[464] In September of 1871, the proprietor of the springs, John M. Armistead, began delivering it by the gallon to private residences in Atlanta.[465]

The streetcar company took notice of the heavy traffic between the city and Ponce de Leon Springs and in 1871, it extended the Peachtree Street line north to what is now Ponce de Leon Avenue and then over a private right-of-way to the spring.[466] To do so they had to build a 270 foot long, 40 foot high wooden trestle over a deep ravine and creek between the present Myrtle Street and Argonne Avenue.[467] According to Garrett's sources, "[i]t was the marvel of the street railway system."[468]

Joel Chandler Harris:

The Constitution added Joel Chandler Harris as an editorial associate in 1876. Famous for his Uncle Remus stories which would later be immortalized into a movie, Walt Disney's *Song of the South*, he would become a household name in Atlanta culture and history.[469]

Two years after joining *The Constitution*, Mr. Harris began including his famous Uncle Remus stories in his columns.[470] Harris was asked to continue a column called Uncle Si, but he did not like the name or the way the column was handled, so he created his own column.[471] Mr. Harris was known in general for his sense of humor. Garrett writes that Mr. Harris brought his family up from Savannah in the summer of 1876 to flee a yellow fever epidemic that had broken out. Even under these trying circumstances, he checked in at the Kimball House as follows: "J. C. Harris, one wife, two bowlegged children, and a bilious nurse."[472]

The History of Washington Seminary, Predecessor to The Westminster Schools:

Washington Seminary, the eventual 'girls school component' of the current Westminster Schools, in Atlanta, had its inception in 1878.[473] The school was founded by Miss Lola Washington and Miss Anita Washington, who were the great-nieces of Lawrence Washington, a half-brother of George Washington.[474]

In 1878, Anita Washington, after graduating from St. Mary's College in Raleigh, North Carolina, came to Atlanta for a prolonged visit with her aunt, Mrs. W. S. Walker.[475] After several weeks, Mrs. Walker suggested that Anita begin tutoring her daughter, Lillie Walker. Later, the younger Walker children also became students, and then neighbors began sending their girls.[476] Anita invited her sister, Lola, to move to Atlanta to assist her.[477] The Walker house was located at "232 West Peachtree Street, on the west side, between Simpson and Powers (West Peachtree Place)."[478] The original name of the school was The Misses Washington School for Girls, despite the fact that the first group of eight students included boys.[479] In 1882, the name of the school was changed to Washington Seminary. By 1886, it had moved to 24 East Cain Street. By 1887, it had relocated to the southwest corner of Walter and Fairlie Streets and by 1900, it had moved to 36 East North Avenue.[480] In 1904, Llewellon Scott and his sister Emma inherited the school and in 1913 purchased a home on Peachtree Street to house the school. In 1953, Washington Seminary merged with The Westminster Schools which was the reincarnation of the North Avenue Presbyterian School which in the spring of 1951 was financially strapped and considering closing.[481]

Defoors Ferry and Johnson's Ferry:

Sadly, two famous roads named after former ferries across the Chattahoochee bear the taint of unsolved crimes.

On the night of July 25, 1879, Martin Defoor, the proprietor of Defoor's Ferry and namesake of Defoors Ferry Road, and his wife Susan were murdered while they slept in their home located on the west side of what is now Chattahoochee Avenue just north of Moores Mill Road.[482] The bodies were nearly decapitated by ax blows and robbery apparently was not the motive.[483] The murder was never solved.[484]

Johnson's Ferry Road also has an intriguing unsolved crime associated with it. William Johnson, the proprietor of Johnson's Ferry Road died and was buried during the second week of December, 1879. On Saturday, December 13, 1879, some friends of the deceased visited the gravesite and noticed that the mound appeared "rough and irregular."[485] Later that day, due to suspicion that the grave might have been robbed, they decided to inter the remains and found that the corpse had, in fact, been removed.[486] An investigation followed immediately thereafter and it was discovered that the preceding Friday afternoon, two men had crossed Johnson's Ferry in a wagon and asked the ferryman the location of Providence Church which is where Mr. Johnson had been buried.[487] The same two men re-crossed the Chattahoochee at Heard's Ferry after dark the same day.[488] The Heard's Ferry ferryman asked the two men about a foul smell which was emanating from the rear of the wagon and was told that it was a drunken colleague who had passed out and vomited.[489] During this period of time, medical colleges were finding cadavers in scarce supply, such that some medical colleges would pay as much as $100.00 for a cadaver.[490] The police, accompanied by the Heard's Ferry ferryman, went to the Atlanta Medical College where the ferryman identified the janitor, George Vaughn, as one of the two men in the wagon.[491] Mr. Vaughn was found guilty of a misdemeanor, although he denied any connection to the crime.[492] The body was never recovered and his grave at Providence Church cemetery remains empty to this day.[493]

James M. Ottley is a 37 year-old real estate lawyer, a fourth generation Atlantan, a resident of Vinings, a humble student of Atlanta history and an ardent admirer of Franklin Garrett and his lifetime of contribution to our city.

All photographs for this book were taken by James M. Ottley.

[1]Garrett, Franklin. Atlanta and Environs: A Chronicle of Its People and Events, Volume I. Athens: University of Georgia Press, 1954; p. 5.
[2]Ibid; p. 1.
[3]Ibid; p. 6.
[4]Ibid; p. 6.
[5]Ibid; p. 24.
[6]Ibid; p. 8.
[7]Ibid; p. 8.
[8]Ibid; p. 8.
[9]Ibid; p. 8.
[10]Ibid; p. 9.
[11]Ibid; p. 9.
[12]Ibid; p. 11.
[13]Ibid; p. 11.
[14]Ibid; p. 11.
[15]Ibid; p. 11.
[16]Ibid; p. 100.
[17]Ibid; p. 100.
[18]Ibid; p. 100.
[19]Ibid; p. 100.
[20]Ibid; p. 100.
[21]Ibid; p. 100.
[22]Ibid; p. 100.
[23]Ibid; p. 25.
[24]Ibid; p. 26.
[25]Ibid; p. 127.
[26]Ibid; p. 127.
[27]Ibid; p. 143.
[28]Ibid; p. 143.
[29]Ibid; p. 162.
[30]Ibid; p. 162.
[31]Ibid; p. 162.
[32]Ibid; p. 162.
[33]Ibid; p. 170.
[34]Ibid; p. 170.
[35]Ibid; p. 170.
[36]Ibid; p. 170.
[37]Ibid; p. 379.
[38]Ibid; p. 379.
[39]Ibid; p. 379.
[40]Ibid; p. 333.
[41]Ibid; p. 333.
[42]Ibid; p. 343.

[43] Ibid; p. 344.
[44] Ibid; p. 344.
[45] Ibid; p. 344.
[46] Ibid; p. 344.
[47] Ibid; p. 352.
[48] Ibid; p. 352.
[49] Ibid; p. 352.
[50] Ibid; p. 424.
[51] Ibid; p. 424.
[52] Ibid; p. 424.
[53] Ibid; p. 434.
[54] Ibid; p. 434.
[55] Ibid; p. 434.
[56] Ibid; p. 434.
[57] Ibid; p. 434.
[58] Ibid; p. 434.
[59] Ibid; p. 946.
[60] Ibid; p. 946.
[61] Ibid; p. 115.
[62] Ibid; p. 116.
[63] Ibid; p. 116.
[64] Ibid; p. 116.
[65] Ibid; p. 117.
[66] Ibid; p. 143.
[67] Ibid; p. 143.
[68] Ibid; p. 145.
[69] Ibid; p. 145.
[70] Ibid; p. 145.
[71] Ibid; p. 145.
[72] Ibid; p. 145.
[73] Ibid; p. 148.
[74] Ibid; p. 149.
[75] Ibid; p. 149.
[76] Ibid; p. 149.
[77] Ibid; p. 149.
[78] Ibid; p. 149.
[79] Ibid; p. 150.
[80] Ibid; p. 150.
[81] Ibid; p. 150.
[82] Ibid; p. 150.
[83] Ibid; p. 183.
[84] Ibid; p. 183.
[85] Ibid; p. 183.
[86] Ibid; p. 183.
[87] Ibid; p. 184.

[88]Ibid; p. 184.
[89]Ibid; p. 185.
[90]Ibid; p. 185.
[91]Ibid; p. 185.
[92]Ibid; p. 185.
[93]Ibid; p. 185.
[94]Ibid; p. 185.
[95]Ibid; p. 185.
[96]Ibid; p. 186.
[97]Ibid; p. 186.
[98]Ibid; p. 186.
[99]Ibid; p. 186.
[100]Ibid; p. 187.
[101]Ibid; p. 188.
[102]Ibid; p. 188.
[103]Ibid; p. 153.
[104]Ibid; p. 153.
[105]Ibid; p. 153.
[106]Ibid; p. 153.
[107]Ibid; p. 153.
[108]Ibid; p. 153.
[109]Ibid; p. 153.
[110]Ibid; p. 154.
[111]Ibid; p. 154.
[112]Ibid; p. 160.
[113]Ibid; p. 160.
[114]Ibid; p. 160.
[115]Ibid; p. 160.
[116]Ibid; p. 160.
[117]Ibid; p. 160.
[118]Ibid; p. 160.
[119]Ibid; p. 160.
[120]Ibid; p. 160.
[121]Ibid; p. 415.
[122]Ibid; p. 415.
[123]Ibid; p. 415.
[124]Ibid; p. 415.
[125]Ibid; p. 189.
[126]Ibid; p. 189.
[127]Ibid; p. 189.
[128]Ibid; p. 190.
[129]Ibid; p. 190.
[130]Ibid; p. 190.
[131]Ibid; p. 238.
[132]Ibid; p. 238.

[133] Ibid; p. 238.
[134] Ibid; p. 335.
[135] Ibid; p. 336.
[136] Ibid; p. 165.
[137] Ibid; p. 191.
[138] Ibid; p. 191.
[139] Ibid; p. 191.
[140] Ibid; p. 191.
[141] Ibid; p. 191.
[142] Ibid; p. 211.
[143] Ibid; p. 211.
[144] Ibid; p. 211.
[145] Ibid; p. 211.
[146] Ibid; p. 211.
[147] Ibid; p. 271.
[148] Ibid; p. 271.
[149] Ibid; p. 271.
[150] Ibid; p. 272.
[151] Ibid; p. 273.
[152] Ibid; p. 272.
[153] Ibid; p. 272.
[154] Ibid; p. 273.
[155] Ibid; p. 266.
[156] Ibid; p. 266.
[157] Ibid; p. 266.
[158] Ibid; p. 266.
[159] Ibid; p. 380.
[160] Ibid; p. 380.
[161] Ibid; p. 397.
[162] Ibid; p. 396.
[163] Ibid; p. 397.
[164] Ibid; p. 685.
[165] Ibid; p. 685.
[166] Ibid; p. 685.
[167] Ibid; p. 685.
[168] Ibid; p. 685.
[169] Ibid; p. 703.
[170] Ibid; p. 703.
[171] Ibid; pgs. 224-225.
[172] Ibid; p. 225.
[173] Ibid; p. 225.
[174] Ibid; p. 225.
[175] Ibid; p. 225.
[176] Ibid; p. 225.
[177] Ibid; p. 225.

[178]Ibid; p. 225.
[179]Ibid; p. 225.
[180]Ibid; p. 225.
[181]Ibid; pgs. 225-226.
[182]Ibid; p. 226.
[183]Ibid; p. 227.
[184]Ibid; p. 227.
[185]Ibid; p. 258.
[186]Ibid; p. 259.
[187]Ibid; p. 259.
[188]Ibid; p. 260.
[189]Ibid; p. 261.
[190]Ibid; p. 265.
[191]Ibid; p. 265.
[192]Ibid; p. 266.
[193]Ibid; p. 266.
[194]Ibid; p. 266.
[195]Ibid; p. 314.
[196]Ibid; p. 315.
[197]Ibid; p. 315.
[198]Ibid; p. 315.
[199]Ibid; p. 322.
[200]Ibid; p. 322.
[201]Ibid; p. 322.
[202]Ibid; p. 360.
[203]Ibid; p. 361.
[204]Ibid; p. 361.
[205]Ibid; p. 361.
[206]Ibid; p. 362.
[207]Ibid; p. 363.
[208]Ibid; p. 363.
[209]Ibid; p. 363.
[210]Ibid; p. 363.
[211]Ibid; p. 365.
[212]Ibid; p. 365.
[213]Ibid; p. 365.
[214]Ibid; p. 365.
[215]Ibid; p. 365.
[216]Ibid; p. 365.
[217]Ibid; p. 410.
[218]Ibid; p. 410.
[219]Ibid; p. 410.
[220]Ibid; p. 411.
[221]Ibid; p. 411.
[222]Ibid; p. 493.

[223] Ibid; p. 494.
[224] Ibid; p. 495.
[225] Ibid; p. 497.
[226] Ibid; p. 510.
[227] Ibid; p. 509.
[228] Ibid; p. 509.
[229] Ibid; p. 509.
[230] Ibid; p. 510.
[231] Ibid; p. 510.
[232] Ibid; p. 520.
[233] Ibid; p. 520.
[234] Ibid; p. 520.
[235] Ibid; p. 520.
[236] Ibid; p. 520.
[237] Ibid; p. 520.
[238] Ibid; p. 521.
[239] Ibid; p. 521.
[240] Ibid; p. 521.
[241] Ibid; p. 521.
[242] Ibid; p. 521.
[243] Ibid; p. 521.
[244] Ibid; p. 521.
[245] Ibid; p. 521.
[246] Ibid; p. 521.
[247] Ibid; p. 521.
[248] Ibid; p. 521.
[249] Ibid; p. 521.
[250] Ibid; p. 522.
[251] Ibid; p. 522.
[252] Ibid; p. 522.
[253] Ibid; p. 522.
[254] Ibid; p. 522.
[255] Ibid; p. 522.
[256] Ibid; p. 522.
[257] Ibid; p. 522.
[258] Ibid; p. 523.
[259] Ibid; p. 523.
[260] Ibid; p. 583.
[261] Ibid; p. 583.
[262] Ibid; p. 583.
[263] Ibid; p. 583.
[264] Ibid; p. 583.
[265] Ibid; p. 583.
[266] Ibid; p. 583.
[267] Ibid; p. 583.

[268]Ibid; p. 583.
[269]Ibid; p. 597.
[270]Ibid; p. 597.
[271]Ibid; p. 597.
[272]Ibid; p. 597.
[273]Ibid; p. 599.
[274]Ibid; p. 600.
[275]Ibid; p. 603.
[276]Ibid; p. 604.
[277]Ibid; p. 603.
[278]Ibid; p. 603.
[279]Ibid; p. 603.
[280]Ibid; p. 603.
[281]Ibid; p. 605.
[282]Ibid; p. 606.
[283]Ibid; p. 606.
[284]Ibid; p. 607.
[285]Ibid; p. 607.
[286]Ibid; p. 607.
[287]Ibid; p. 612.
[288]Ibid; p. 612.
[289]Ibid; p. 638.
[290]Ibid; p. 638.
[291]Ibid; p. 639.
[292]Ibid; p. 639.
[293]Ibid; p. 612.
[294]Ibid; p. 612.
[295]Ibid; p. 612.
[296]Ibid; p. 613.
[297]Ibid; p. 613.
[298]Ibid; p. 613.
[299]Ibid; p. 614.
[300]Ibid; p. 614.
[301]Ibid; p. 615.
[302]Ibid; p. 615.
[303]Ibid; p. 615.
[304]Ibid; p. 615.
[305]Ibid; p. 615.
[306]Ibid; p. 615.
[307]Ibid; p. 615.
[308]Ibid; p. 615.
[309]Ibid; p. 617.
[310]Ibid; p. 617.
[311]Ibid; p. 617.
[312]Ibid; p. 621.

[313]Ibid; p. 622.
[314]Ibid; p. 621.
[315]Ibid; p. 621.
[316]Ibid; p. 621.
[317]Ibid; p. 626.
[318]Ibid; p. 626.
[319]Ibid; p. 627.
[320]Ibid; p. 628.
[321]Ibid; p. 628.
[322]Ibid; p. 629.
[323]Ibid; p. 633.
[324]Ibid; p. 633.
[325]Ibid; p. 633.
[326]Ibid; p. 634.
[327]Ibid; pgs. 634-635.
[328]Ibid; p. 635.
[329]Ibid; p. 636.
[330]Ibid; p. 639.
[331]Ibid; p. 639.
[332]Ibid; p. 640.
[333]Ibid; p. 640.
[334]Ibid; p. 642.
[335]Ibid; p. 649.
[336]Ibid; p. 649.
[337]Ibid; p. 649.
[338]Ibid; p. 651.
[339]Ibid; p. 651.
[340]Ibid; p. 652.
[341]Ibid; p. 652.
[342]Ibid; p. 661.
[343]Ibid; p. 953.
[344]Ibid; p. 953.
[345]Ibid; p. 679.
[346]Ibid; p. 679.
[347]Ibid; p. 701.
[348]Ibid; p. 701.
[349]Ibid; p. 701.
[350]Ibid; p. 701.
[351]Ibid; p. 711.
[352]Ibid; p. 711.
[353]Ibid; p. 725.
[354]Ibid; p. 725.
[355]Ibid; p. 725.
[356]Ibid; p. 726.
[357]Ibid; p. 726.

[358]Ibid; p. 727.
[359]Ibid; pgs. 883-884.
[360]Ibid; p. 884.
[361]Ibid; p. 661.
[362]Ibid; p. 662.
[363]Ibid; p. 662.
[364]Ibid; p. 728.
[365]Ibid; p. 728.
[366]Ibid; p. 923.
[367]Ibid; p. 923.
[368]Ibid; p. 745.
[369]Ibid; pgs. 752-753.
[370]Ibid; p. 753.
[371]Ibid; p. 753.
[372]Ibid; p. 754.
[373]Ibid; p. 754.
[374]Ibid; p. 841.
[375]Ibid; p. 884.
[376]Ibid; p. 884.
[377]Ibid; p. 842.
[378]Ibid; p. 865.
[379]Ibid; p. 865.
[380]Ibid; p. 865.
[381]Ibid; p. 865.
[382]Ibid; p. 865.
[383]Ibid; p. 865.
[384]Ibid; p. 914.
[385]Ibid; p. 876.
[386]Ibid; pgs. 876-877.
[387]Ibid; p. 878.
[388]Ibid; p. 878.
[389]Ibid; p. 891.
[390]Ibid; p. 891.
[391]Ibid; p. 891.
[392]Ibid; p. 892.
[393]Ibid; p. 914.
[394]Ibid; p. 935.
[395]Ibid; p. 935.
[396]Ibid; p. 940.
[397]Ibid; p. 940.
[398]Ibid; p. 940.
[399]Ibid; p. 940.
[400]Ibid; p. 764.
[401]Ibid; p. 764.
[402]Ibid; p. 764.

[403] Ibid; p. 764.
[404] Ibid; p. 764.
[405] Ibid; p. 764.
[406] Ibid; p. 764.
[407] Ibid; p. 765.
[408] Ibid; p. 765.
[409] Ibid; p. 765.
[410] Ibid; p. 771.
[411] Ibid; p. 777.
[412] Ibid; p. 775.
[413] Ibid; p. 788.
[414] Ibid; p. 789.
[415] Ibid; p. 805.
[416] Ibid; p. 805.
[417] Ibid; p. 830.
[418] Ibid; p. 814.
[419] Ibid; p. 814.
[420] Ibid; p. 815.
[421] Ibid; p. 815.
[422] Ibid; p. 815.
[423] Ibid; p. 815.
[424] Ibid; p. 815.
[425] Ibid; p. 815.
[426] Ibid; p. 838.
[427] Ibid; p. 838.
[428] Ibid; p. 838.
[429] Ibid; p. 838.
[430] Ibid; p. 838.
[431] Ibid; p. 838.
[432] Ibid; p. 838.
[433] Ibid; p. 839.
[434] Ibid; p. 842.
[435] Ibid; p. 842.
[436] Ibid; p. 843.
[437] Ibid; p. 843.
[438] Ibid; p. 843.
[439] Ibid; p. 846.
[440] Ibid; p. 846.
[441] Ibid; p. 846.
[442] Ibid; p. 847.
[443] New Georgia Encyclopedia. "Oglethorpe University." 8/24/2004. UGA Press. <http://www.GeorgiaEncyclopedia.org>; p. 3.
[444] Ibid; p. 3.
[445] Garrett, Franklin. Atlanta and Environs: A Chronicle of Its People and Events, Volume I. Athens: University of Georgia Press, 1954; p. 863.

[446] Ibid; p. 863.
[447] Ibid; p. 863.
[448] Ibid; p. 863.
[449] Ibid; p. 863.
[450] Ibid; p. 863.
[451] Ibid; p. 863.
[452] Ibid; p. 863.
[453] Ibid; p. 863.
[454] Ibid; p. 863.
[455] Ibid; p. 863.
[456] Ibid; p. 881.
[457] Ibid; p. 881.
[458] Ibid; p. 881.
[459] Ibid; p. 881.
[460] Ibid; p. 881.
[461] Ibid; p. 881.
[462] Ibid; p. 881.
[463] Ibid; p. 881.
[464] Ibid; p. 881.
[465] Ibid; p. 881.
[466] Ibid; p. 883.
[467] Ibid; p. 883.
[468] Ibid; p. 883.
[469] Ibid; p. 927.
[470] Ibid; p. 928.
[471] Willis, Christian E., "Song of the South." 1999. <http://www.SongoftheSouth.net>; p. 2.
[472] Garrett, Franklin. Atlanta and Environs: A Chronicle of Its People and Events, Volume I. Athens: University of Georgia Press, 1954; p. 928.
[473] Ibid; p. 943.
[474] Ibid; p. 943.
[475] Ibid; p. 943.
[476] Ibid; p. 943.
[477] Ibid; p. 943.
[478] Ibid; p. 943.
[479] "Washington Seminary." The Westminster Schools, Atlanta, Archives. <http://www.Westminster.net>; p. 1.
[480] Garrett, Franklin. Atlanta and Environs: A Chronicle of Its People and Events, Volume I. Athens: University of Georgia Press, 1954; p. 943.
[481] "History." The Westminster Schools, Atlanta, Archives. <http://www.Westminster.net>; p. 1.
[482] Garrett, Franklin. Atlanta and Environs: A Chronicle of Its People and Events, Volume I. Athens: University of Georgia Press, 1954; pgs. 959-960.
[483] Ibid; p. 959.
[484] Ibid; p. 959.
[485] Ibid; p. 961.

[486]Ibid; p. 961.
[487]Ibid; p. 961.
[488]Ibid; p. 961.
[489]Ibid; p. 961.
[490]Ibid; p. 961.
[491]Ibid; p. 961.
[492]Ibid; pgs. 961-962.
[493]Ibid; p. 962.

Made in the USA
Columbia, SC
18 December 2019